THE GOSPEL ACCORDING TO TED LASSO

REV. MATTHEW TITUS

Second Edition
Copyright © 2023 Rev. Matthew Titus

Scripture taken from the Common English Bible Web Site®, Copyright ©2012 by Common English Bible and/or its suppliers. All rights reserved.

All rights reserved. No part of this book may be reproduced or transmitted in any form by any means, electronic, mechanical, photocopy, recording or other without the prior written permission of the publisher. For information on getting permission for reprints and excerpts, contact: Rev. Matthew Titus at pastormtitus@outlook.com

ISBN: 978-1-960705-00-6

https://www.pinnlead.com/pl-press

DEDICATION

This devotional is dedicated to Erin,
Ashleigh, and Miriam.

CONTENTS

	Acknowledgments	i
1	How to Engage This Book	Pg 1
2	What is *Ted Lasso*?	Pg 5
3	Pilot	Pg 7
4	Biscuits	Pg 21
5	Trent Crimm: The Independent	Pg 31
6	For the Children	Pg 39
7	Tan Lines	Pg 49
8	Two Aces	Pg 57
9	Make Rebecca Great Again	Pg 67
10	The Diamond Dogs	Pg 81
11	All Apologies	Pg 91
12	The Hope That Kills You	Pg 97

ACKNOWLEDGMENTS

For all those who were very curious about this show and were not judgmental about my constant optimism regarding it. Thank you, you helped me put this together in more ways than you can imagine.

Specifically, I'd like to thank a few friends and colleague who helped encourage me, focus my work, provide insight, and just reveled in this show with me. In no particular order -

Michael, Philip, Jason, Stephanie, Lexanne, Kimi, the congregation of the Lutheran Church of The Redeemer, Mary, Mark, Ariel, and Erin.

1
HOW TO ENGAGE THIS BOOK

Every devotional has its own flow and cadence. Each devotional you get to use can and should impact you in specific and distinct ways. Of course, every devotional should not be approached the same way for they all serve different purposes and are geared towards different audiences. Below, I briefly describe several approaches to using this book, recognizing readers may discover even more.

This devotional can be used in either an individual or group setting, but I typically prefer to use this in a group setting. The way I process things is by talking to others. So, naturally being in a group setting is my own personal preference. Talking with others allows us to help solidify our own thoughts, we can benefit tremendously by hearing the thoughts and voices of others as they pick up on nuances and see connections we haven't seen, and finally, as people of faith it is *good* to be gathered together. As Coach Lasso says towards the end of the first season of *Ted Lasso*, "you are not alone."

What I found to be the most helpful way to approach a group study with this material is to watch an episode together and just enjoy the show. Don't worry about note taking or connections you see. Just watch for enjoyment.

After the show, it might be good to have a brief discussion about the things within that episode that were most enjoyable to you or brought on questions. This is an opportunity to get those surface level thoughts out of the way.

Use this time to discuss a particularly good joke, moment, or scene with the group. It can also be a great time to get some clarification on a point that you might have missed. Use this after watch discussion to just talk about how much you enjoyed (or didn't enjoy) the episode. In this moment don't worry about faith and religious connections.

I always enjoy taking a few days to process things that I've watched. So, schedule a time to gather with your group a few days later to discuss those faith connections that you and the group saw. You are welcome to use the discussion questions at the end of each chapter to help guide conversation. However, the first question should be something like, "Where did you see God in this?"

By no means do I believe that the material I've written here is an exhaustive list of faith connections. Your group might either see God at work in ways that this book doesn't discuss or might see God at work in deeper ways than I've written here. Both are wonderful experiences that you will get to have!

During the study I've done with my congregation we would gather on Thursday evenings for a watch party that lasted no more than 45 minutes. Someone gives a brief 'catch-up' about what has happened in previous episodes, and we give space for discussions about the show after the episode is over.

I encourage the group to think about that episode for the next few days. If they want to watch it again, they are welcome to do that on their own time. We would then gather again on Sunday afternoon for the faith discussion. This gathering typically lasted about 45 minutes to an hour depending on how much the gathered group spoke.

Obviously, youR group size can alter how long each session is. But, if you also decide to establish this Thursday/Sunday model, you've got at least a 10-week Faith Study, and who doesn't love that?

Finally, here are some helpful tips when introducing this show to people who have never seen it before:

- Make sure people know about the language and adult material used and discussed in this show.
- Encourage people to participate *at least* for the first four weeks. *Ted Lasso* is the type of show that builds over time and becomes stronger.
- Remind people that they don't have to know *anything* about soccer to enjoy *Ted Lasso*.
- Turn on subtitles; especially for those audiences who are not accustomed to hearing English spoken with many different accents.
- Remind people that this is a show that is authentic and real, but also doesn't follow the same sports stereotypes that we've become accustomed to in film and television.

Lastly, remember to have fun. God has given us imagination, laughter, and emotions to enjoy and experience life to its fullest. *Ted Lasso* is an exceptional show full of heart, warmth, positivity, authenticity, and love.

Have fun, because if something isn't fun why would you keep on doing it?

2
WHAT IS TED LASSO?

Ted Lasso has quickly become one of my favorite television shows of all time. I find myself watching episodes and seasons multiple times, either by myself or inviting others to watch with me. With each viewing, I can't help but smile, laugh, and cry as I see God at work through these beautiful characters.

This is one of those shows everyone should watch. It is one of the most heart-warming, genuine, and positive shows that has come out in a very, very long time. Jason Sudeikis and Bill Lawrence have helped create a show that turns sports tropes on their head and has subverted how we might view the world.

The show's titular character, Coach Ted Lasso, quoting Walt Whitman, compels you to 'be curious, not judgmental.' Be curious about this show and all it offers. It doesn't matter if you don't typically enjoy sports movies or you know nothing about soccer/football (don't worry, Ted is firmly in that camp with you), you will find enjoyment in this show.

But, what is it about exactly? For starters, it is a show that follows an American football coach as he is hired to coach a fictional English

Premiere League soccer team. The reasons as to *why* he is hired to manage this team with almost no knowledge of the sport is reason enough to watch the show itself. The ride it'll take you on is memorable and like a kid a theme park, you'll want to hop back on that ride to experience it again and again.

Ted Lasso helps us see that appreciating others, listening to people, and lifting up other's strengths is a wonderful way to engage life and those around you. It is in those positive and delightful moments where there is a large amount of overlap into how Jesus calls us to live this life of faith.

Jesus invites us into a life that is lived for others, that declares you *good enough* already, and in which you are never alone. Jesus reminds us that you are loved, accepted, forgiven, and sent out into the world to proclaim that message to any and all you encounter through your words and actions in life.

The ministry of Jesus and the lessons lived out by Coach Lasso fit nicely together. What follows in this book are what I see as the most obvious and interesting overlaps between this faith that I live and this show that I love. I do not believe that this is an *exhaustive* list, and I'd love to talk to anyone about other glimmers of the gospel they might notice in this show.

If you haven't seen the show yet, I encourage you to go and watch the entire first season, and then come back and check this book out as you get to watch it again and again.

I hope and pray that you will find as much enjoyment, fun, and moments where God is at work that I and so many others have.

3
PILOT

NEW VENTURES

> ***Ted Lasso*** - *Are we nuts for doing this?*
> ***Coach Beard*** - *Yeah, this is nuts!*

Coach Theodore "Ted" Lasso and Coach Beard board a flight from the United States to England to coach AFC Richmond – a premier league football club. Neither of them has any experience coaching this sport as they are more accustomed to the American gridiron football. As Ted says in his first press conference, "You could fill two internets with what I don't know about football." They are off to a new venture and journey, pushed and pulled by their innate desire to coach, mold, and inspire athletes to perform their best and become better humans along the way.

Throughout their journey in this first episode (and throughout this first season of *Ted Lasso*) there are those who will consistently tell them that they are doing something monumentally, 'mental.' They are told they are out of their element and they don't belong. Most of the time, those who share their opinions with them – especially to Ted – don't do so very warmly.

Yet Ted, with Coach Beard at his side, continues dancing and doing what he loves and feels is the very core of his own identity: coaching others.

Throughout scripture, there are moments — plenty of them — where the brief exchange that Ted and Coach Beard share could be repeated among the faithful that God has chosen, guided, and is choosing to come alongside out of love. Abraham and Sarah[1], Mary and Joseph[2], and the disciples of Jesus[3] are clear examples. Each of them could ask one another, 'Are we nuts for doing this?' More often than not, the answer would still be the same. 'Yeah, this is nuts.'

Abraham goes on a journey to a land he's never seen (and brings along his whole family and community with him), Mary and Joseph endure the stares and the shame as they parent *the* son of God, the disciples follow the one whom they believe to be the Messiah.

What each of them does and did *is* nuts. Many would and have labeled them as 'mental' for what they felt called to do. And yet... they still venture forward. They are buoyed in the faith that God is with them, guiding them, and caring for them. They desire to share with any and all they encounter this experience and story, inviting others into that journey as well.

Our God sends each of us out to places and to people and to circumstances that others might scoff at, ridicule us for, and at times be downright hostile towards. God invites us to live life in a way that is *different* from what others expect or even how the world operates. We know that even when we feel called outside of our comfort zones, we'll be OK because God is not only with us, but God's love is present as well. We are called to share that love, that mercy, that life with

---

[1] Genesis 12
[2] Matthew 1: 18-25, Luke 2:1-40
[3] Matthew 4:18-22

all we meet. Even and especially when it takes us to places we'd never expect.

The Gospel According to Ted Lasso

HONESTY AND AUTHENTICITY

> ***Rebecca Welton*** *– Well?*
> ***Ted Lasso*** *– You know, I always figured that tea would taste like hot, brown water. And you know what? I was right. It's horrible. No thank you.*

One of the more surprising things about Ted Lasso is that he's incredibly honest. He tells you like it is with a smirk and a smile on his face. However, this isn't like how we've seen 'brutal honest' portrayed in other shows, movies, or books. He isn't trying to be mean, demeaning, or sarcastic.

He's just being honest, even when what he is sharing isn't always the best news to share. When he agrees to take some tea from Rebecca, he already figures he isn't going to like it, but he tries it anyways. When she asks his opinion, he doesn't hold back.

In the simplest ways, we see that Ted is an *authentic* person. He gives you exactly what he intends and doesn't hide who he is from anyone, not even his new boss.

- - - -

There is a story[4] that is shared by Jesus about when a man of considerable wealth approaches him and states that he's done *everything* to be good in God's eyes. He's followed the commandments and doesn't treat anyone else in a poor way. But, he still asks, "What must I do, if I've already done everything else?"

Jesus' response to him is both honest and authentic. He affirms this man and says that he indeed has kept true to his ability to follow the commandments. The one thing he lacks is that he should sell his possessions and give them to the poor. After he does that, he should come and follow him.

---
[4] Matthew 19:16-30, Mark 10:17-27, Luke 18:18-27

This man is said to have gone away grieving because he had many possessions and would find it difficult to give them up and give them away.

Jesus isn't being mean or condescending to this man. He instead is being honest and authentic. The man is told that there is more to life than clinging to what people think is valuable and that he needs to turn away from that life and follow the one who has come from God.

Being able to say, "I'm happy that you like this, but it isn't my thing," is a *good* thing to share.

What would life be like if we were able to be more honest and authentic with one another?

Our honesty does not mean trying to dominate, humiliate, or take advantage of anyone, but being authentic in the way we express ourselves, so that everyone might know how we're feeling.

BEING KNOWN

> **Ted Lasso** – You continue to impress, Nate.
> **Nathan Shelley** – You remembered my name.

As the kitman, the one who tends to all the equipment of AFC Richmond, Nathan Shelley is on a low rung when it comes to the hierarchy of the football club. He doesn't get to make decisions like the owner and manager, he doesn't get to be cheered and glamorized like the players, he doesn't even get fawned over like the partners and spouses of the players; no, he sits right at the bottom. His responsibilities rest in making sure the uniforms are clean, the boots are in top shape, and the pitch is well cared for. Because of his low stature in the organization, he's accustomed to not being known.

Yet, he is the very first person working for AFC Richmond that Ted and Coach Beard meet. He's not used to being talked to by upper management, nor being treated so kindly and on an equal level. He is so accustomed to his place within the club that he doesn't even know how to respond when Ted asks his name.

Nate is surprised and begins to be the first to 'fall into' the Lasso Way because through Ted he experiences what everyone desires – to be known.

- - - -

It is *good* to be known. One of the most important stories[5] of our faith comes in John's gospel as Mary Magdalene is tending the tomb of her friend and savior. Of course, this is after the resurrection and the tomb is empty. In her grief and pain from the last three days, she doesn't recognize that Jesus is standing before her and mistakes him for a simple gardener. Jesus *knows* her, calling her by name. When he says, "Mary!" she instantly knows that this is the one who *knows* her with her fear, grief,

---
[5] John 20: 1-18

and loneliness vanishing in an instant.

All of creation desires to be known. When you walk into your classroom on the first day of school, start a new job, or join a new team, the first thing you want is for someone to know who you are. All of us want that; there isn't a person on the planet who doesn't hope that someone knows who they are.

We get to follow a God who *knows* us. From being known in our mother's womb to knowing every hair on our head, our God *knows* us. Our God has claimed us in love and grace. There is nothing we have done to receive that love, and there is nothing we can do to lose that love. We *already* have it.

Nate didn't do anything to be remembered by Ted, he is remembered because Nate is important enough and good enough to be remembered. Just as we are important enough and good enough already to be known by our God and our Lord.

POTENTIAL

> ***Ted Lasso*** *– Smells like potential. And am I getting notes of AXE Body Spray?*

At his very core, Ted Lasso is a coach. He isn't an American football coach, and he surely isn't a Premier League football coach, he is *a coach*. Coach Lasso loves to guide, shape, and mold another person so that they can achieve their best in whatever they seek to do well.

Ted's calling as a coach rests in the *potential* he sees not only in the athletes he gets to manage, but in every person with whom he interacts. He has the brilliant ability to not only squeeze out top-level performance in each person under his charge through affirmation and positive reinforcement, but he truly believes that whoever is before him can be better because *they are better*.

He sees potential in the shy Nathan Shelley, the loud Keeley Jones, the gruff Roy Kent, and even the arrogantly gifted Jamie Tart. He sees the unbridled potential in each of them, that not only will make those athletes better on the pitch, but will allow each of them to see how truly wonderful and gifted they are as humans.

- - - -

All of scripture begins with the story of Creation[6]. This beautiful story of God creating something out of nothing; separating the waters, light, and land. God fills all of creation with *stuff* – plants, animals, birds, insects, *life*. God even fashions humanity in God's own image, formed to steward and care for all that has already been created.

At the end of each 'day' of creation, God emphatically states that *it is good*. What has been created is *good*. The beings – all of them – with life breathed into them – are *good*. Very good.

---

[6] Genesis 1

Throughout scripture, God knows the potential of life *because it is good*. Even when things go astray and awry, God continues to see the potential in what has been created. Yet, God knows that something *more* needs to be done to drive this point further home. So, God desires to be one among creation so that they might know, fully and completely, how their – how our – potential rests in the knowledge that we are *good*.

God is made known in and through the person of Jesus, the one who directs our attention away from all that draws us from the goodness of God. Jesus is the one who continues to do so, even when we become distracted, because our *potential* rests in the fact that we are already *good* in God's eyes; inviting us to live into that goodness that already rests in us because we have been created by God.

THE ALLURE OF SIN

> ***Rebecca Welton*** *– I want to torture Rupert...in a constant loop...like a GIF.*

As we are introduced to Rebecca Welton, the new owner of AFC Richmond, we can tell that there is something deeper and possibly more sinister behind her desire to hire a new manager for her football club. The viewer begins to suspect that there is something more to Rebecca's hiring of this new manager – who has never coached this particular brand of football – as the whole world is shocked by this decision. We get to hear and see their surprise shown through a segment of ESPN announcing this new hire and even through the fan who talks to Ted on the flight that brings him to England.

Throughout the episode, we are shown hints of how her ex-husband hurt her and damaged their marriage because he never *truly* cared about it or even fully loved her as his wife. Near the end of this episode, she explains her 'plan' to Higgins, her 'right hand' in her role as owner, that she wants to destroy this club because it will destroy her ex-husband.

Beneath her cheery and supportive façade lies a desire and a hunger to hurt someone who has truly hurt her. No matter who she hurts along the way, as long as she enacts revenge, she believes she will have 'won.'

- - - -

Sin has a way of worming into our hearts and lives. Many times, sin is lived out 'just because' and because we have the power and the ability to do it. The story of David and Bathsheba is one of those simple stories of sin.

King David[7] wants someone for himself – as he peers from his roof at Bathsheba. He lusts after her and enacts a plan to 'have' her all to himself. No matter who he hurts along the way, he's going to get what he wants,

---
[7] 2 Samuel 11:1 – 12:15

and no one is going to stop him.

That allure of sin is prominent within our lives. It can and does entice every person within creation. More often than not, we learn to rationalize and justify our sinful desires because we feel we 'deserve' what we seek — power, wealth, lust, revenge — and partly because it can come *so easily* to us. If it wasn't this easy, it'd be wrong, right?

I believe our God knows how enticing sin is and how easily we can fall prey to it, so God has committed Godself to turn us away from that which sends us into spirals of hurt, shame, and pride. Our God is constantly reaching out in ways that show us that there *is* another way. Rebecca has Higgins, Keeley, Ted, and others who will continue to be that guiding light of God shining through them telling her that there *is* another way to live. Just as we have our friends, family, and community where God works in and through to care for us, love us, and guide us away from all that pulls us from the goodness of God.

DISCUSSION QUESTIONS

- When have you felt called to do something 'mental?'
    - What kept you moving?
    - What kept you *from* moving?
- Have you ever been truly honest with someone?
    - What made it easy or difficult?
- How well do you receive honest critique?
    - Why do you think that is?
- In what ways does knowing someone's name help establish a relationship?
- How important is it for someone (or an organization) to know your name?
- What does it mean for you to be known by God?
- How much do you see yourself the way that God does, 'being good enough?'
    - Why or why not?
- Why do you think sin is so tantalizing for us?

4
BISCUITS

BISCUITS. CAESAR SALAD. CAKE.

> **Ted Lasso** – *I brought you a little something. Yeah, cookies. Or as y'all call them here, biscuits.*

Ted starts a tradition with Rebecca on his first full day as the new manager by bringing her delicious biscuits, using that time for them to bond and to get to know one another. Ted is explicit that this is a gift *for her* and he's going to continue to show up each day, no matter what.

Throughout this episode, food plays a central role. Whether it is the biscuits, the lunch that Higgins and Ted have together, the hamburger that Ted helps Keeley eat at her photoshoot, or the food for Sam's birthday party, all of it centers around relationships. Building, cultivating, listening, and learning.

Ted's use of food is that bridge into other people's lives, helping him show that he is on equal footing with those around him. Whether he is offering it to others, sharing it, helping serve, or having fun; Ted uses food to begin and deepen those relationships in his life.

- - - -

Food plays a pivotal role within the life of faith in the Christian Community as well. In fact, food plays a vital role within all aspects of life within creation. Sharing a meal with another person or a group of people is an intimate experience and shows how close people can be.

Friends at a coffee shop, a first date at a fancy restaurant, a messy table surrounded by family, a ladle of food scooped for those in need – all of that and more can define and deepen our relationships with those around us.

In each of the gospels, Jesus invites his friends and followers to a Passover[8] meal, but at this meal he shifts it just a bit to show how important *this* meal will be. This simple meal of bread and wine is something *more*. This food – this life of God – is offered *for you*. We continue to share this meal together as we gather as a people of faith.

This meal of bread and wine, of body and blood, is given and shed *for us* as we remember that our God shares life with us. We get to receive this meal given freely for all who come to the table. This meal gathers people from all facets of life around the table reminding us that we are *all* invited to this feast.

---

[8] Matthew 26:17-30; Mark 14:12-25; Luke 22:7-20; John 13:1-30

KNOWING, NOT UNDERSTANDING

> **Trent Crimm** – *I'm curious, could you explain the offsides rule?*
> **Ted Lasso** – *Well Trent, I'm going to explain it the same way the US Supreme Court did back in 1964 when they defined pornography. It ain't easy to explain, but you'll know it when you see it.*

Always trying to catch their team's new manager in a less than stellar fashion, the local media continually tries to make Ted look like a fool. For most of those looking from the outside in, he is a fool. He doesn't understand the complexities of the game he is coaching, nor does he understand some of the basic rules. What's funny about this question is that everyone has their own 'twist' on what offsides actually means and looks like. However, Ted knows that being a good coach doesn't mean you need to 'know' everything about the game, as long as you have people around you to help guide you. Ted has Coach Beard and the kitman – along with all the players on his team – and the countless individuals who give him 'advice' in the community.

- - - -

One of the most foundational aspects of the Christian faith is the tenet of the Trinity – the belief that God is and always has been three persons – Father, Son, and Holy Spirit. Each is equal, but all are different. For even the smartest and most faithful of individuals, trying to fully understand the Trinity can make your brain hurt.

There have been those throughout history who have tried to 'explain' it in somewhat simple terms, but each explanation falls just a bit or wildly off from what the Trinity actually is.

But, understanding the Trinity is not a prerequisite for being *loved and cared for* by God[9]. There is no test that one must pass in order to be 'fully

---
[9] Romans 8:31-39

included' in God's love and life. There are no hoops one must jump through to experience God's love.

Of course, there will always be those who will attempt to get you to 'pass' their tests, but much how Ted describes the offsides rule, you can be held firm in the fact that, 'you'll know God's love when you see it and feel it.'

Not What We Expect

Keeley Jones – *What would you rather be, a lion or a panda?*

What would you rather be? For many, the obvious answer is a lion. They are depicted as proud and majestic animals that 'rule' the lands they roam. They can be fierce, strong, and beautiful; who wouldn't want others to see them that way?

Yet, Ted says he'd rather be a panda. Curiously he never gives a reason as to why, but he seems pretty certain that, for him, the panda is the better animal to be. Perhaps it's because they don't seem to worry about living up to any sort of preconceived image. Maybe it's because pandas get to sit around and eat a lot. Who knows, but Ted's answer to this question strikes us as odd, leading us to ask other questions, mainly, "I wonder how the world looks through his eyes?"

- - - -

Throughout our faith history, there have been stories about who the messiah would be and how they would present themselves to the world.

Would the Messiah be a mighty warrior, come to lay final waste to all of God's enemies? Would the Savior possess words that would be used to definitively convince all to come and follow God? Would the One be some cosmic figure that no one could look upon and have any doubt about who they were?

If anything can be agreed upon about Jesus, it would be that Jesus is none of those things. He isn't a warrior; his words, though intriguing to many, haven't definitively convinced all of creation; and he hasn't presented himself in such away with awe, power, and might that would cause even the most dubious to change their mind.

God has a tendency to work in a *different* way[10]. Instead of all that, we get

---

[10] Matthew 1: 18-25; Luke 2:1-40

a son of a young woman and her carpenter husband, who travels the countryside with intriguing stories, deep questions, and a promise that God already loves even the most pushed aside groups of people in society.

Jesus – and the stories that foretell his coming – are not what the world expects. He leads us to ask more questions and we become more intrigued by who this person is. Jesus opens us and our hearts to opportunities to get to know not only him, but the message he shares more deeply.

A Team

> **Ted Lasso** – *Jamie, I think that you are so sure that you are one in a million, that sometimes you forget that out there, you are one of eleven.*

We have all heard that there is no "I" in team and Ted (like any coach) believes that through and through. What is interesting in his approach about conveying that to his star athlete, Jamie Tartt, Ted doesn't use ridicule or power. Instead, he tries to remind him that even though he is great at this sport (and he *is great,*) that his full potential as an athlete will only be fully realized when he allows his game to work with his teammates. If Jamie learns to share those moments of glory and athletic skill with those around him, the team can achieve greatness together.

- - - -

Paul visited, interacted with, and wrote to many new church communities during his travels. Paul did so much to share and spread this message of God's love and presence and how life changing that message can be (as it was for him).

One of his great messages was to the church in Corinth as he talked about the church body and how it compares to the human body[11]. An individual part of the body cannot say to another, "I have no need of you." All of the body works together to give life and health to the entire body. It can't all be an ear or an eye or a mouth. Each part of the body is vital and integral to the whole.

The same is true for the church body – the Body of Christ. We might not all possess the same gifts, but we work together to bring wholeness, wellness, support, and love to the entire body. We work in tandem to achieve life and live into love.

---

[11] 1 Corinthians 12:12-31

When one part of the body hurts, we work together to heal it. When one part of the body does well, we work together to celebrate.

We are all in this together, serving with and for one another so that all might be cared for in life.

DISCUSSION QUESTIONS

- What kind of meal do you always share with a new person in your life?
    - Does it matter what type of relationship it is – romantic, friendship, or work related?
- Are you more of a 'sit down and eat' person or a 'need to stay on the move' person?
    - What are the advantages and disadvantages of those ways of eating with others?
- What are some things that you *know*, but don't quite understand?
    - Is it easier knowing things or understanding them in life?
- How do you react when someone gives an unconventional answer to a question?
- Is it easy for you to work with a group?
    - What role do you like to take in those groups?
    - What role do others typically see you filling in those groups?
- If the answer to the previous two questions is different, why do you think that is?

5
TRENT CRIMM: THE INDEPENDENT

LET THE CHILDREN COME

> **Ted Lasso** – I think it's really cool you do this.
> **Roy Kent** – Only doing it 'cause my fucking niece goes here.
> **Ted** – Oh yeah? Which one is she?
> **Roy** – That idiot.

For all his gruffness, stand-off demeanor, grunts, and growls, Roy Kent is a caring and sensitive individual. The way he interacts with his niece is precious and priceless. It is not just how he acts towards her, but how he interacts with all her classmates at school as well. He is encouraging, engaging, and kind to every child he meets. In many ways, he's more like Ted than he even knows.

Roy cares *enough* about these children that he takes more time to be with them than others typically would. He wants them to know that they are special and good. In the same way, Ted wants to make sure everyone knows that as well.

Throughout history, children have unfortunately not been universally treated well. More often than not, they are ignored, thought to be unimportant, and more times than we can imagine are not considered to be 'real people' until they too can bear children and contribute in a more substantial way in the community.

Many look at children and think they are needy, whiny, and sometimes annoying. But, in actuality they are just little versions of all of us. We once were children too. We needed time to grow and learn. We needed opportunities to learn from others and model our lives based on how we see others being treated.

Jesus doesn't see children as an annoyance. Jesus doesn't consider children to be 'less than' in any way. Jesus seeks them out, he heals them when they are in need, he gathers what they offer, and he desires them to learn from him.

There are probably many who wouldn't agree with the language that Roy uses around children (especially his own niece), but no one can deny that he cares for them, wanting them to have fun, and for each of them to know that they are good enough.

Jesus wants the same and more for the children of the world. Jesus calls us to be *like* children as we come to the faith with an open heart and an innate joy to live.

Knowing All of Who You Are

> *Roy Kent* – *I mean, what even is A Wrinkle in Time?*
> *Trent Crimm* – *It's a lovely novel. It's the story of a young girl's struggle with the burden of leadership as she journeys through space.*
> *Ted Lasso* – *Yeah. That's it.*
> *Roy* – *Am I supposed to be the little girl?*
> *Ted* – *I'd like you to be.*

One of the most unusual and most precious gifts that Ted possesses, is his is ability to know the people around him – really understand them in way that they might not be able to see. He wants them to understand the goodness and the gifts that they possess. So, he gives all of his players a book that he believes will help them see those gifts more clearly in themselves. For Roy, whom he wants to be the leader to rally everyone to his way of coaching, that means identifying with the young girl in *A Wrinkle in Time*.

Sometimes the hardest thing is realizing the gifts you possess; it takes someone else to point it out and share it with you. Ted is excellent in sharing what he sees in his athletes and the people around him.

One of the more well-known conversations that Jesus has involves a woman he meets at a well[12]. This is a meeting that crosses many societal boundaries of that day and time and there is *a lot* that goes on within this brief exchange that is only inferred. However, within this conversation Jesus is able to tell this woman many things about her that others wouldn't know. Most importantly, he sees a gift of proclamation and speaking and instructs her to go and tell her village all about him and what he has to share.

---
[12] John 4:1-42

She obliges and becomes the first preacher of Jesus' message to others.

Each of us possesses gifts and skills that sometimes we might not be able to see in ourselves. It might be because we don't believe the world will see the value in it, others might not agree with what we have to say (simply because it is coming from a person others might see as 'less than'), or we just might have doubts that we possess anything to give.

No matter what, we believe in a God who sees value in everyone. We believe in a God who truly loves everyone. You have gifts *because* God has gifted all of us. Sometimes it takes listening to those around us to know those gifts. You never know, someone might see a great strength within you that you never thought anyone would see.

You have gifts and skills. You can use those gifts and skills to continue to proclaim God's love to everyone.

Getting to Know You

> ***Trent Crimm*** *– And though I believe Ted Lasso will fail here and that Richmond will suffer the embarrassment of relegation, I won't gloat when it happens. Because I can't help but root for him.*

In a sly attempt to divide and enrage the fanbase of AFC Richmond, Rebecca Welton taps Trent Crimm from The Independent to do an expose on Ted Lasso. Though Crimm is given more than he could ever ask for in writing an article detailing how little this new coach knows about football, he cannot help but be intrigued by this man. Even though he feels deeply that the 'Lasso Way' will not succeed (because it is so wildly different from how it has been done before), he cannot help but enjoy Ted as a person and as a coach.

Ted has a way of making you feel known, appreciated, and listened to. Even if he doesn't know all the things you know, he enjoys spending time with you and is excited about getting to invite you into the way he views the world. Thankfully, Ted's view of the world is drastically different from how others have typically viewed the world.

- - - -

In the gospel of Mark[13], Jesus sends his disciples on a mission where they are to proclaim God's love and Word, heal those in need, and invite everyone to repent from all that draws them away from God. Before they return from that journey, there is a rather odd story that is placed right in the middle[14].

It doesn't involve Jesus. In fact, he's not really alluded to at all in this short story, but it does involve John the Baptist and his time in prison at the demand of Herod Antipas.

Herod imprisons John the Baptist because he's a thorn in his side. John the

---

[13] Mark 6:6b-13
[14] Mark 6:14-29

Baptist proclaims a word, a message, and a view of life that is *different* from what is normally said. In fact, he continues to point his proverbial finger at those like Herod – those in power who take advantage of others and don't lead a life that God has given them. However, though Herod is always *upset* with what John the Baptist has to say, he is greatly intrigued by what he does say. So much so, that he wants to keep this 'strange man' around.

The Word we get to proclaim as people of faith *is different* from the world. It really is. Because of its difference – caring for others over yourself, supporting those on the margins, listening to all because they are worthy to be listened to, believing that at our very core each person is already loved by God – there are many who will disagree with the broadness of the message, but are intrigued by the many parts.

DISCUSSION QUESTIONS

- Be honest, how do you typically view children?
    - Why do some view them more positively or negatively in life?
- What is something you do for your family that others might think is 'out of character' for you?
- Share a moment when someone saw something about you that you couldn't see.
    - What about a time when you were able to do that for someone else?
- What makes it difficult to talk and share about your faith with others?

6
FOR THE CHILDREN

DIFFICULT CONVERSATIONS

> ***Roy Kent*** *– I'm switching tables.*
> ***Ted Lasso*** *– No, no, no. Hey. Come on back here. I parent trapped y'all. Take a seat.*

From the moment you begin watching *Ted Lasso* and are introduced to Roy Kent and Jamie Tartt, you know that they do not like one another. Roy is a seasoned veteran at the end of his career, and Jamie is the young phenom who doesn't want anyone to stand in his way.

Both men and athletes are incredibly similar. They believe that their way of approaching football is *the best* way. They are both a little jealous of each other. They are both frustrated that their team's season is not going the way that they'd hope.

Add in the dynamics of age and youth, opposite personalities, and differing humor, and you've got a powder keg waiting to explode.

Of course, Ted would like his star players to at least tolerate one another so that the team could start playing better together. So, at the team's charity auction and dinner, he encourages/forces them to have a conversation and see where each one is coming from.

- - - -

There is a text in the Gospel of Matthew[15] that has been wildly misattributed for a long time. Now, it doesn't mean that *how* it's been used is incorrect, it's just that from the context in which the verse is taken doesn't apply to how people use it today. That text is Matthew 18: 20 – *For where two or three are gathered in my name, I'm there with them.*

Typically, you'll see that verse used in the context of a small worship setting. Implying that even though the gathering is small, Jesus is still present among those worshippers. Of course, Jesus is *always* present among those worshipping him, Jesus is present with you – the reader – right now as you read this devotional.

However, what this gospel verse actually refers to is when we are having *difficult* conversations with those who have upset us. All the verses preceding Matthew 18:20 are about what the followers of God should do when someone has hurt them with their words or actions.

Talk with them one on one, bring in a few un-biased witnesses, bring the issue to the community. This specific verse pertains to the fact that even when a small group is having those tough, but needed, conversations, Jesus is right there with them as support and guidance.

I don't believe Jesus *wants* us to be at one another's throats in anger and hostility. Jesus desires us to work as one in order to continue to proclaim God's love and to serve those in need in the world. Yet, Jesus acknowledges that discrepancies exist, giving us a model and guide to follow when those differences make an appearance in our relationships.

Remember, even when there is a small group gathered having difficult

---

[15] Matthew 18:15-20

conversations in order to make whole what has been broken and torn in a relationship, Jesus is right there too.

Freed

> **Nathan Shelley** – I just wanted to say thanks for talking to Colin and Isaac.
> **Roy Kent** – Why is your face so close to mine?
> **Nathan** – Well, my initial plan was to hug you, but I just chickened out just now.

As mentioned before, Nathan Shelley occupies a very low spot within the hierarchy of AFC Richmond. What tends to happen in our fallen and off-kilter world to those who are seen as 'beneath' others is that they are picked on, made fun of, and taken advantage. Nathan Shelley, unfortunately, is subject to that tried and true aspect of humanity. He is picked on, a lot. Two players – Isaac and Colin –do so because they are trying to get into the good graces of AFC's young phenom, Jamie Tartt.

With the subtle influence of Ted Lasso, Roy Kent desires to put a stop to those antics because he sees Nathan as an integral part of the team. He doesn't like it when others are bullied.

Liberated into newfound freedom, Nathan wishes to express his gratitude to Roy, but also knows that Roy is not one for 'sentimental emotions.' But, in the end Nathan's freedom and the joy of emotion it causes is too much for him to hold, wrapping Roy up in a fierce embrace.

– – – –

Nathan experiences freedom, *true* freedom within the AFC Richmond locker room. This freedom will allow him to grow exponentially, become more confident in himself, and be a more trusted asset to the team as a whole. This freedom allows Nathan to truly be who he was created to be.

Whenever we as people of faith talk about freedom, we don't mean the type of freedom that others associate with that word. The freedom we experience – gifted to us in the life, death, and resurrection of Jesus – doesn't give us the ability to do anything we want, whenever we want, however we want. That is a selfish freedom, a freedom that doesn't think about others and only concerns itself with one's own desires and wants.

No, the freedom that our faith proclaims is a freedom to *serve* others. It is a freedom granted because we don't have to worry about measuring up to anyone anymore. We *know* that we are already good enough. There is nothing that can remove that freedom from us. In response to that freedom and love, we are called and invited to serve others through care, grace, forgiveness, and love.

In that freedom we get to grow into the people that we have been created to be. Our God walks with us in those moments and guides us into that service. Like Nathan showing affection and love to Roy, we too get to shower our love upon God because in God's eyes, we are good enough.

Good enough to be free. Good enough to serve. Good enough to grow.

It's Not All About Looks

> **Rebecca Welton** – *All the way from outside… please welcome Cam something.*

We are introduced to Cam Cole very briefly in *Ted Lasso* earlier in the season. He is a street musician outside where Ted and Coach Beard live. His looks are *different*. His musical setup is *less than* ideal. And yet, he always has someone willing to listen to him sing and play.

For an event like the 10th Annual Benefit for Underprivileged Children gala and auction, Cam Cole *does not* fit. Where everyone in attendance is dressed exquisitely, Cam is dressed in rags by comparison. His instruments all look like they were picked up out of a trash pile and appear barely functional.

Yet, once Cole starts playing, all those hesitancies of the posh gathering evaporate as they begin to listen, dance, and enjoy themselves.

- - - -

John the Baptist was weird[16]. He is weird for us in this modern age as we read of his description and actions, while he was just as weird for those who experienced him firsthand.

John the Baptist was *not* what folks had in mind when they thought of a prophet of God. John the Baptist would scream and yell from the edge of the traditional community, calling for people to repent and turn back to God. His hair was unkempt, his clothes were ragged, and he ate less than appetizing food.

Yet, when he spoke, he spoke with an authority and care people hadn't heard before. His message was so enticing that many, many people gathered to hear him and to be washed by him in the Jordan River.

---

[16] Matthew 3:4, Mark 1:6

God used this unusual man to usher in and announce God's in-dwelling in creation. He is used to begin the ministry of God's Son, Jesus who is the Christ.

It wasn't about looks or appearances, but about what was being offered.

We could learn a lot from both of these stories. Making sure that we are not swayed by the culture of the world, but instead willing to listen to the content of what someone has to offer. May it all lead us closer to the one who has created us.

DISCUSSION QUESTIONS

- How do you feel when you have difficult conversations with others?
    - Why?
- Where do you see God present in those hard moments?
- How would you define freedom?
    - Are there limits to that freedom?
- What do you think keeps you from living into the freedom that God offers us in and through Jesus?
- When was a moment in your life that you judged a person simply based on their looks?
    - How were you surprised by that individual?
- What sorts of things feed our ability to judge a person by how they look?

7
TAN LINES

THE LOVING FATHER

>**Nathan Shelley** – *That is a lot longer run than he thinks though.*
>**Coach Beard** – *Metaphor.*

As we roll into this fifth episode of *Ted Lasso,* we begin to learn that the titular character, though always seemingly full of sunshine and happiness, isn't immune to struggles of his own. At the beginning of this episode, we discover that Ted and his wife, Michelle, are having marital issues stemming from his constant optimism.

Despite those difficulties and stresses, Ted is filled with anticipation and joy to see his wife and their son, Henry. He is so preoccupied with their arrival that he has already run into a door when he wasn't paying attention to where he was going, and now, as he sees their successful and safe arrival, he runs the entire length of the pitch in order to meet them. In essence, Ted makes himself look like an emotional fool.

The underlying message of all this is to show that Ted's love and joy for his family – even in the midst of his own struggles within those relationships – is more important than what anyone else thinks.

- - - -

In the Gospel of Luke[17], Jesus tells a story that many of us have heard titled as 'The Prodigal Son.' This story about the return of the son who has wasted and squandered all that has been given him. In this story, Jesus emphasizes how this 'wasteful' son is not only welcomed back, but celebrated in the embrace of his father. However, that only tells a small portion of this parable and might not be the exact (or at least the exclusive) point that Jesus is trying to make.

The story involves two brothers and the father's love for both of them. This loving father is willing to meet them where they are to show how deep and wide his love for them extends. The father gives the younger son what he asks for (even if what he gives makes him look weak), celebrating that son's return, running to meet him and wrapping him up in a hug full of love and hope even before this son could apologize for all that he's done wrong. Finally, the father meets with his older son who is jealous and dealing with his own feelings of not living up to his father's love and not being celebrated in that love in quite the same way.

Each time the father shows his love, he is doing so in a way that the prevailing culture of that time (and more than likely our time; too) would view as weak, foolish, and unbecoming of a parent and a person of high stature. Yet, this father's love and joy for his family supersedes what the world thinks, so that his family knows where they stand in his life – always with him.

This unconditional love is how our God views us. Our God runs in a full sprint to meet us, celebrating our mere presence, and meeting us where we are in our hurt, anger, and confusion. Our God does this no matter what the outside world might think. The love that Ted shows his family is only a small fraction of the love that God has for you and for all creation.

---

[17] Luke 15:11-32

OKLAHOMA!

> **Ted Lasso** – What's wrong?
> **Michelle Lasso** – Nothing. I think I'm just a little jet-lagged is all. I-I'm fine, Ted.
> **Ted** – No, no, no, no. No. Michelle, you gotta talk to me. Okay? Hey, hey. Oklahoma.

As AFC Richmond are on the verge of winning their first game under the leadership of Ted Lasso, Ted begins to see the positive investment he's put into his team begin to pay off. In that work, he can also see that the change his team needs involving tough decisions (removing Jamie Tartt from the game) are similar to the tough decisions he needs to make within his own personal life regarding his marriage with Michelle.

That needed personal change began with a marriage counselor giving Ted and Michelle a 'code word' to use so that they could be completely honest with one another. That word, 'Oklahoma,' meant that the next response had to be completely truthful between them – no matter what it was.

That truthful response helped them not only know one another better, but it also began to open their eyes – especially Ted's – that something drastic might have to be done in order for them both to be truly happy. This is very similar to how his decision to remove Jamie Tartt from the game meant that no player, no matter how talented they were, could get in the way of making the team function together as a unit.

As painful as both the decision to remove Jamie and the decision to consider ending his marriage are, they were the correct decisions to make.

- - - -

Many of Jesus' parables begin with a 'code phrase,' "You have heard it was said…" When Jesus spoke those words, you knew that his next words would be totally honest and would completely flip on its head what the prevailing world view on a topic.

The way God approaches life, at times, is different from the way the 'world' would want you live. Where the world might say take, God says give. When the world says, 'care for yourself first,' God invites us to serve our neighbor in need. When the world calls for people to 'fall in line,' God is there, at times, to shove a stick in the wheels of injustice so that the world might take a new, better, and healthier path.

All of that comes with drastic changes that focus on *others* before they focus exclusively on ourselves. This is learning to think of yourself as part of a greater whole, where if the whole is cared for, you are cared for as well. Ted was able to do that with his family – thinking of Michelle's happiness so that her life could thrive – as well as his team.

God continues to proclaim that love and service in creation. Whether you hear someone yell, 'Oklahoma!' or utter 'You have heard it was said...' know that what follows might be completely honest, but it's an honesty rooted in love and care for you, for others, and for the world.

A BIT DIFFERENT

> **The Crowd** – *Wanker! Wanker! Wanker!*
> **Coach Beard** – *You hear that, Coach?*
> **Ted Lasso** – *Well, same word, ain't it?*
> **Coach Beard** – *Yeah, but different.*

The most colorful term used against Ted as he takes the helm of AFC Richmond is, well, wanker. As he explains to his son, 'that's a man who likes to be alone with his thoughts.' Being called that isn't really a term of endearment. It means essentially, a person who is 'wasting another's time.' The whole fandom of AFC Richmond object to Ted as their team's coach because they think it is a waste of time and that he isn't going to help them at all, only furthering to hurt their team and its perception among the Premier League as a whole. So, they let their displeasure be heard, quite often.

Yet, after AFC Richmond's first win under Ted's leadership, the crowd continues to chant that same word, but as Coach Beard puts it, it is *different*. It is chanted as a term of endearment and camaraderie. It is an acknowledgement that maybe Ted isn't such a 'waste' as they initially thought, even if he does do things wildly different than what they are used to seeing and experiencing.

During Jesus' ministry within the world as he walked around Galilee and the surrounding areas, that whole area was occupied by the Roman Empire. The Roman Empire was a brutal regime that kept the people it had conquered in line through fear and intimidation. The Pax Romana (the peace of Rome) was at times quite literally held in place with nails and wood.

That is, the nails and wood of the cross.

The cross was an instrument of corporal punishment. It is where the supposed worst of the worst were sentenced by the Roman government to die. Their death was not peaceful, but was instead agonizing as they endured the pain of nails through their limbs, slowly struggling to breathe as they were suffocated upon the cross by their own body.

On top of that agony, their death was public. People gathered to see these 'criminals' die. Some of those criminals were violent and had caused horrible tragedies, but many were political criminals, used as an example to keep the people in line.

If you speak out against the occupiers; you risk the pain and shame of the cross.

Jesus was sent to the cross, not because he caused destruction or death among his fellow people, but because he spoke out against the worldly powers of his day – the Roman Empire and the religious elite – who took advantage of the vast majority of the population. He was publicly executed in a shameful and shame-filled death on the cross.

And yet, through his death and resurrection, the cross has taken on a new meaning. No longer is it seen as simply a form of torture and execution, but instead as something that cannot hold the power and love of God down. The faithful who have followed Jesus and claim him as the messiah have repurposed this tool of death as a sign of hope and salvation.

For it is on the cross that God's love is poured out and that victory over sin and death is shown. The cross no longer is something to be feared, instead transformed into a sign of hope. In this victory of God over sin and death, we see that the cross is empty, where death does not reside anymore. The cross cannot hold down what God continues to lift up and set free; new life and love. What the Roman Empire meant as torture and insult, God, in and through Jesus, transformed into peace and affirmation. God continues transforming the world, including us, even now.

DISCUSSION QUESTIONS

- Who do you typically identify with in the parable of The Loving Father/Prodigal Son?
    - Why do you identify that way?
- How might changing the name of this parable affect how you read it?
- How do you typically view change in your life?
- What are the words and phrases you hear that make you pay better attention to what someone is saying?
- Have you ever heard of the cross described as an instrument of torture and death before?
    - How does that make you feel?

8
TWO ACES

Righteous Anger

Jamie Tartt *– Relax, Ted. It's just practice.*

Jamie Tartt is 'hurt.'

On any other day and with any other athlete, I believe that Ted would believe him and would not want one of his athletes to further injure themselves. However, he knows that Jamie is not physically hurt, but his pride is hurting because he was taken out of the previous game. So, Jamie is refusing to practice with his team because his ego has been harmed.

Ted, for obvious reasons, is not OK with this attitude. Again, Jamie is thinking about himself more than his teammates. Ted never uses improper language; he doesn't demean Jamie. Yet, in his anger – and he is angry – he continues to remind Jamie that this isn't acceptable, and Jamie knows it isn't acceptable.

– – – –

In one of Jesus' most well-known miracles[18], he raises Lazarus from the dead. He calls him out of the tomb and Lazarus stumbles out, still wrapped in his burial clothes. It's a powerful story showing all those gathered and those believing today that the mere voice of Jesus has power and authority. Jesus' voice is enough to turn back death and bring back life.

However, before Jesus shouts for Lazarus to 'come out' of the tomb, he looks around at those who are mourning and grieving their friend's death and grows upset. He's angry. In seminary, I had a classmate who translated this part of John's gospel as Jesus being, 'pissed in spirit.'[19]

Jesus is filled with a saddened anger because the people around him, the people who have told him through their words, actions, and prayers, those who believe him to be the messiah cannot understand the hope and life that is with them. Jesus is frustrated that even with all these people have seen and proclaimed, they still don't have the trust that he hopes they would.

What I love most about Jesus' saddened anger is that it shows how much he truly cares. Just as Ted's anger towards Jamie's antics shows how much he *actually* cares about this team and about each person on that team, Jesus cares enough about who he is for the world that he's willing to get angry.

And yet, in that anger Jesus doesn't push people aside, he doesn't give up, he doesn't lash out and hurt others. No, Jesus sees the death and mourning around him and with just words brings life from that death. He brings joy from that sorrow.

---

[18] John 11
[19] John 11:33, '…he was *greatly disturbed in spirit*…'

Pure Joy

Dani Rojas – *Nanananana! Dani Rojas, Rojas! Dani Rojas!*

The first time we meet Dani Rojas, Richmond's transfer player from Mexico, he is full of life and energy. As Ted Lasso calls him, he's a 'beautiful, raven-haired golden retriever.' He exudes positivity and optimism. He truly enjoys what he gets to do – play football.

That kind of infectious positivity rubs off on everyone around him. He also doesn't horde that feeling just for himself but includes everyone in his effort to be the best footballer. Even when he his competing with Jamie, he cannot help but radiate joy and encouragement.

His infectious joy is *good* because it is authentic. He isn't putting on a show. He isn't being something he is not. He's just being himself – lovable, positive, welcoming, and encouraging. He's also open to learning and growing. What more could you want?

- - - -

I have a saying in my ministry, "We live a life of get to, not have to." We get to live this life of faith. We get to worship God. We get to serve with and for one another. We *get to* do so much in, with, and through God's love.

We don't *have* to do anything. Once something turns that corner and becomes a *have to* it begins to look like a chore. It begins to become something you don't look forward to doing. When you *have* to do something, it becomes less fun to be a part of.

Obviously, all of life cannot be that way all the time. However, being able to shift our view from 'have to' to 'get to' can fundamentally change how we approach our lives of faith. A life where, like Dani Rojas, we rush in looking for ways that we can be a part of what's going on. In this life where we share all that we have and all that we are with others; we are always looking to find ways to learn and grow deeper in this faith and service.

I have a friend and colleague who would end each worship service with – "Go in peace and serve the Lord. And have fun doing it, because if it isn't fun, why would you want to do it?"

There is so much to love and enjoy in this life of faith; there really is. We *get* to live this life of faith because of what God has done, is doing, and will do through love and grace.

SACRIFICE

> ***Sam Obisanya*** — *Wait, so, Coach, how do we fix this? We can't change the past.*
> ***Ted Lasso*** — *No, Sam. No, we cannot. But we can choose to honor it. Now, those young men, they made the ultimate sacrifice. So, I think it's only fair that we sacrifice something of our own.*

There is a story from AFC Richmond's history, that back during World War I, many flyers went up encouraging young men to try out for their favorite team to become professional footballers. However, the flyers were a ruse to draft more men to the burgeoning war effort. Four hundred men enlisted that day, and very few returned home to their families. Since that day, the training room inside Richmond's stadium has been 'haunted' and no one tries to use it.

Unfortunately, the Greyhound's newest ace, Dani Rojas, does receive treatment there and then is mysteriously 'hurt' on the field during an individual practice. Many theories arise as to how Dani was hurt and *who* caused his injury. The team begins to freak out and lose its newly acquired 'cool.'

In response to this situation, Ted asks his team to offer up something special to them as a sacrifice to 'appease' the ghosts of those young men who sacrificed their lives. All members of the team let go of those items they find special — a beloved pet's collar, sand from a beach, cleats, and even keys to their car. A true bonding experience comes from this, and the team begins to *finally* begin working as a true team.

- - - -

Take up your cross and follow me[20].

Those are words spoken by Jesus to his disciples and to all those gathered

---
[20] Matthew 16:24-26; Mark 8:34-9:1; Luke 9:23-27

around him. In those words, Jesus is telling those who follow him that the life that he is inviting them into isn't going to always be easy. There will be times of struggle, hardship, and some might even die for what they believe.

I remember leading a Sunday School class once where the group was pining for 'the better days' of the past when people would just show up to hear about God. This individual commented about how they felt that the church was welcoming and kind with the doors wide open. So, where were the people? Another individual chimed in and said, 'Maybe we need to do more than just open doors, but to go out and be with people and lead them here.'

Doing something like that involves sacrifice, sacrificing your time and your pride. In this life of faith, we are called to go outside comfort zones to be with people where they are.

That is what this life of faith calls us into and that is the life that our Lord has invited us to be a part of. Living this life of faith has so many benefits – knowing that you are loved, including other voices in your life because of God's hospitality and welcome working through you, seeing yourself as part of a greater whole than ever before, and so much more. And yet, living that sort of life at times is at odds with the world and culture around us. Living this life of radical love, inclusion, and generosity while serving with and for those in need can put people at odds with you.

We will sacrifice a lot, but we will gain so much more in the end.

Take up your cross and follow me. Living this life that Jesus invites us into isn't always easy, but I believe it is always worth it.

FOOTBALL IS LIFE

> ***Dani Rojas*** *– Coach? Football is life.*

AFC Richmond is dealt a major blow within their locker room when, arguably, their best player is given back to Manchester City. Jamie Tartt is no longer on Richmond's squad.

After all the work that Ted has done to get through to Jamie – finally getting him to believe into what Ted is trying to build in this team – he's gone. Naturally, the coaching staff is distraught. Ted was looking forward to having 'two aces' on the pitch. That potential future is now gone.

Seeing that his coaches are wallowing, Dani Rojas knocks on the door and speaks his signature line, "Football is life." But, this time it isn't with the same joyous exuberance like he's uttered it countless times before. This time, it is said in way that evokes a sense of 'this stinks; but we'll be OK.'

It is exactly what Ted needs to hear. This stinks; but football is still to be played. The future is open and not set in stone.

Have you ever wondered what the most faithful verse in all of scripture is? Have you ever pondered about who might be shown to trust God the most in the Bible? If you're like me, you've definitely thought about that. Most people would say Noah, or Moses, or Mary. But, there is a moment in John's gospel that – for me – speaks to what faith really is.

Jesus has been away from some of his friends, and while he was gone another friend who was not with them died. The family is reeling with grief as Jesus comes to be with them in their mourning. One of Lazarus' sisters, Martha, looks at Jesus, through mournful anger and says, "If you had been here my brother wouldn't have died."[21]

---

[21] John 11:20-21

Those are impactful words. Martha is hurting and yet she knows that with the one she knows to be the messiah, this wouldn't have happened. I imagine that those are similar words that each of us has uttered in our own grief at the loss and death of someone we loved. Yet, she quickly takes that thin step from anger to hope as she speaks what I think is the most faithful saying in all of scripture, 'but even now I know that whatever you ask God, God will give you.'

Those three words – *but even now* – are words of faith and hope. Simple words, but words full of faith. Martha is able to recognize the reality of the moment of her suffering.

Her brother Lazarus has died, her family and friends are mourning, she is filled with so many emotions, but even now she can recognize the hope that Jesus brings and can offer. Even through her struggle, she knows that her Lord and God is right there with her.

She hasn't been left out. Lazarus isn't forgotten. Her community – though grieving – is still held together in and through God's love.

There is so much that we go through each day. As a pastor, I've been witness to so much hurt and grief. I've been honored and humbled to be with people on some of their worst days. Seeing these people's faith close at hand is awe-inspiring.

As we move through hardships in life, let us live into those faithful words of Martha, 'but even now…'

Discussion Questions

- When is it appropriate to be angry?
- Where are some other moments from scripture where Jesus is angry?
    - Why or why not might it be helpful to see this side of Jesus?
- What is something you love to do?
    - Why do you love it?
- Have you ever truly sacrificed something in your life for another person?
    - What was that like for you and for them?
- How do you typically view those who sacrifice things in their life for other people?
- What are ways in your life where you could utter (or have uttered) those faithful words of Martha, 'but even now?'

9
MAKE REBECCA GREAT AGAIN

EVEN TED HAS BAD DAYS

> **Ted Lasso** – What the hell are you doing?
> **Nathan Shelley** – I'm – I'm so sorry. I just -
> **Ted** – You're what? What is this?
> **Nathan** – It's just my thoughts on the team.
> **Ted** – Go, Nathan. Come on, it's past curfew. Go! Get outta here!
> **Nathan** – Sorry.

Ted has had a bad night. His marriage is ending, and his wife is apparently giddy at that new future. However, as Ted mentioned a few episodes before, he never wants to be seen as a 'quitter.' So, he's having a tough time coping with this very real and imminent future.

When we are angry, others usually end up in our crosshairs, and who happens to be the target of Ted's rage? The one and only Nate the Great.

Nathan has written what he thinks the team needs to hear and he's trying to decide whether to share that information with Ted. Ted has given him confidence that he's never had before, allowing him to finally believe in himself. Nathan is seeing himself as a vital part of this team who has a voice and opinion that should be heard.

Unfortunately, as Nathan is trying to share this newfound voice, he catches Ted at a less than stellar moment and is harshly reprimanded for being at Ted's hotel door after curfew. Ted yells at him, sends him away, and doesn't even bother to read Nathan's notes.

Thankfully, the next morning before the match against Everton, Ted apologizes to Nathan, realizing what he did and said was uncalled for and unfair.

There is a story in the midst of the gospels where Jesus seems to have had *enough* of the people around him. Tired, hungry, frustrated, or coming to the realization of what he must do in order to *truly* make himself known to the world, Jesus comes off as a jerk to a particular woman[22] who sees him for who he truly is. She sees Jesus as *the one*. She recognizes he's not just the one for Israel, but for all of creation.

This woman belongs to a group that is 'outside' God's chosen people. She's a Canaanite, a Gentile. She's not a part of Jesus' people. But, she has enough faith in who Jesus is that she comes forward and asks for help.

Jesus appears to disregard her, dismiss her, and treat her just like any other upstanding individual within that culture. He sees her – initially – as someone not worth the time.

Yet, this woman believes that Jesus is the Messiah because she has heard the stories about him. She very well may have been witness to the healings of Jesus which would have strengthened her belief. Her faith is incredibly strong. She's heard and seen how he has lifted up those who

---

[22] Matthew 15:21-28

are cast down and she believes that he is speaking to her as well. This new confidence drives her to approach him and ask for his help.

Her faith *changes* Jesus' mind. In their very brief conversation, Jesus sees and knows that who he is called to be is something more than what he might have initially thought. Seeing her faith, so raw and full of power in the midst of even the Messiah dismissing her, causes Jesus to shift and become *even more welcoming* than he was before.

God's love in and through Jesus is an ever-expanding circle. You are included in that growing circle of welcome and love. Every time a barrier or wall is erected, here comes God to smash it to pieces so that love and welcome can continue to thrive. Not even God's own son can stand in the way of that over-flowing grace.

WHAT THEY NEED TO HEAR

> **Ted Lasso** – *Also, I read through your thoughts.*
> **Nathan Shelley** – *Yeah.*
> **Ted** – *They're great. And I agree with every last one of 'em. But, I can't say this to them.*
> **Nathan** – *But they need to hear it.*
> **Ted** – *I agree. That's why you're gonna do it.*

After Ted's bad night, he apologizes to Nathan and informs him that while his thoughts on the team are really good, he couldn't relay that information to them. Nathan needs to say it to them.

What proceeds may be the most unexpected pre-game talk that I've ever seen portrayed in a sports movie or television show. No matter how unconventional it is, it is *exactly* what the AFC Richmond squad needs to hear before facing Everton.

Nathan speaks with brutal honesty to various members of the team. In that moment they don't just see him as 'one of the team,' but they acknowledge that he is a leader among them. He is an unexpected leader, but someone with true authenticity and passion.

Ted helped build that up in Nathan and it shines through wonderfully.

- - - -

God has a habit of taking unexpected individuals and shaping and molding them into needed leaders. Scripture is full of these great leaders from unassuming places. We have been told the stories of leaders like Noah[23], Abraham[24], and Moses[25]. We have seen leadership spring forth in Mary[26], Thomas[27], Peter[28], and Paul[29]. There are many, many more people as well.

---

[23] Genesis 6:1 – 9:29
[24] Genesis 12:1-23:20
[25] Exodus 2:1-4
[26] Luke 1:26-27
[27] John 11:16

What we end up seeing is that none of those individuals saw those gifts of leadership in themselves. It took God knowing them fully and seeing that they do in fact possess those abilities to lead others.

Each of them held on to their faith despite the opinions of others. There are quite a few who fell *far* from their expected leadership roles, but were still looked to by God to live into what they had been created for.

The beauty of leadership is that more often than not, someone sees those gifts in you before you can acknowledge them for yourself. God works through others to show us that we *do have gifts*.

Nathan would never have recognized what he was capable of unless Ted saw that in him. I believe that each of us have been gifted by God with skills and abilities to help proclaim, nurture, serve, and form those around us in and through God's love and grace.

Sometimes, most of the time, someone needs to see that within us first and be willing to trust us enough to lead others.

---

[28] John 21:15-17
[29] Acts 9

IN THEM ALL ALONG

> ***Roy Kent*** *– Oi! Listen up! None of you are going back to the hotel tonight. 'Cause we did something today that no one thought we could, including us!*

At long last, after more than half a century, AFC Richmond beat Everton. It was something that they didn't believe they could ever do. Add to the fact that their best player, Jamie Tartt, was no longer with them and the odds of them winning any future games seemed to crumble around them.

However, with the help of Nathan Shelley, the unorthodox coaching of Ted Lasso and Coach Beard, and working together as a complete and trusting team, they were able to finally get over that hurdle.

It feels good, and why wouldn't they celebrate that?

- - - -

My favorite story from the gospels must be the Emmaus Road[30] story. This after resurrection story from Luke's gospel helps me remember that no matter what, Jesus is present with us – even when we cannot see him.

Two disciples are in the throes of agony and mourning. They have witnessed the death of the one they believed to be the savior of the world. It has been three days since he died, and they are now making the long and sorrow-filled trek from Jerusalem to Emmaus.

While on the way, they encounter a man they don't recognize. As they talk about their weekend experience, this man begins to share with them all that scripture has talked about and points to. They plead for this man to stay with them. As they are about to eat, the man breaks bread and shares it with these two disciples. In that moment of breaking bread, they realize that the one who had been walking with them the entire time was Jesus himself.

---

[30] Luke 24:13-35

They are not alone. Jesus is alive, and he has been with them the entire time. Filled with new hope and life, they run back up to Jerusalem to share this wonderful news.

The warmth of God's love burned within them as they traveled and spoke to Jesus on the road and shared a meal with him. They run back to their friends. They celebrate the good news of Jesus' resurrection.

Own Up to the Part You Played

> ***Rebecca Welton*** *– God, that man took so much from me.*
> ***Flo 'Sassy' Collins*** *– No. Rupert is a horrible man who built an ivory tower he kept you captive in. But, you climbed every single step of that tower on your own. You're the one who stopped coming home, stopped calling, who made a six-year-old girl wonder what she'd done wrong. I'll always been your biggest defender, but you have to own up to the part that you played.*
> ***Rebecca*** *– You're right.*

Rebecca was captive in a terrible marriage that truly changed who she had always been. No longer the funny, goofy, and caring person she was, she turned into a cold, no-nonsense individual. She pushed the people she cared about away from her as she attempted to live up to the image that her ex-husband desired her to be.

Like many people would, she solely wants to place that change in her upon Rupert, her cruel and narcissistic ex-husband. However, her friend Sassy reminds her that she still played a role in that change. She is still – and always has been – the one who has made decisions in her life. As bad as Rupert was and is, he didn't keep her from reaching out to her family and friends; Rebecca is solely to blame for that. And she is reminded that she must accept and repent from those actions.

Martin Luther had a great way of depicting how we live as people in the world, that we are *simul justus et peccator,* which is Latin for (roughly) "we live as sinner and saint at the same time."

We are not all fully good, but we are also not fully sinful. Both sinner and saint reside in each of us. But, things don't *cause* us to sin – not in the sense that sin makes decisions for us. When given the option to do the easy thing, or the right thing, we tend to do the easy thing.

Of course, we'd love to hang all that blame upon the easy thing. It made me do it, it caused me to choose it. In actuality, we made that decision.

Repentance requires us to acknowledge that we have sinned. John the Baptist called for the people gathered around him to hear his words to not only turn back towards God, but to *repent* from the lives they were living. John called people to acknowledge that they *had sinned*.

Rebecca tried to hang all the blame upon Rupert, but Sassy was there to remind her that she played a pivotal role in all that had transpired during their marriage. However, she was still loved and always will be.

Even in our repentance (and even when we fail to repent), we remember that God *does love us*. No matter what. We repent, not so that we receive God's love, but we repent *because* God's love is already with us.

Rebecca is able to repent because she knows Sassy (and many, many others) are there with her. They love her, care for her, and support her.

So too does God continue to abide with us as we turn away from all that draws us from God.

Panic Attack

> ***Rebecca Welton*** – *It's okay. Try to breathe.*
> ***Ted Lasso*** – *I can't. I don't know what's going on. I'm – I'm sorry.*
> ***Rebecca*** – *It's okay. You're having a panic attack. Just breathe.*

In the middle of his team's celebration as Rebecca is giving a wonderful rendition of *Frozen's* "Let it Go," Ted begins to feel odd. His vision becomes tunneled, there's ringing in his ears that overtakes the sounds around him, his hands become clammy and shaky. As he makes his way out of the night club, he sits down and leans against a wall. Ted has finally hit his stress limit. The compounding pressure of his ending marriage, being away from family, being in a foreign country, and coaching a sport he doesn't know much about catches up to him. Ted experiences a panic attack.

Even though Rebecca has contributed heavily to this experience – and she knows it – she comes to his comfort and aide. Telling him it's going to be alright, and that he is no more 'crazy' than anyone else. She is able to calm him down and get him to focus on what's before him at that moment. She helps get him back to a place where he can go back to his hotel room and rest.

- - - -

Life can be difficult. As I was once told, we are all just a few stressors away from feeling like everything is crumbling around us. There is not a person on this planet that has never felt overwhelming stress and panic. We have all felt those overpowering pressures to measure up and to meet the expectations of others. Those weights we place upon our shoulders and the burdens that others wrap us up in can be suffocating at times. No one is immune to that.

Not even our Lord Jesus is immune to that feeling. As he approaches his impending trial and death, Jesus has to take a moment[31]. He is overcome with stress, anxiety, and perhaps even a bit of fear knowing what is going to happen to him in the next few days.

As he prays for comfort and God's presence with him, he begins to sweat blood. Jesus is freaking out.

And that's OK. That's a lot of weight to carry upon his shoulders.

In his prayer, he is able to calm himself, focus, and lean into God's presence and love with him and through him. In this prayer, Jesus is able to breathe.

There is *no one* who is immune to stress. We all experience it. Even the seemingly most 'put together' people we know have moments where everything seems to fall out of control.

Focusing on who and whose we are (God's very own) helps each of us to center, calm, and bring some needed peace at that time. Know that, like Ted, none of us are crazier than anyone else. Just breathe. You are okay.

---

[31] Luke 22:39-46

DISCUSSION QUESTIONS

- When you are angry, how do you act towards others?
- What pulls you out of those angry episodes?
- When have you been looked to lead others?
    - Is this something you felt prepared for? Why or why not?
- Share a moment when God was with you in the moment, but you could not see that till later.
- How has living up to another person's image of you changed how people have always known you to be?
    - Was this change seen as 'good' or 'unauthentic?'
- What does it mean for you to be a 'sinner' and a 'saint?'
- Why might it be hard for us to acknowledge that we do sinful things?
- Have you ever experienced a panic attack before?
    - If you are comfortable sharing, what did it feel like for you?
- Do you think Jesus experienced a panic attack during his prayer in Luke 22?
- If so, how does that make you feel about Jesus?

10
THE DIAMOND DOGS

F*riends*

> ***Nathan Shelley*** *—I must say that this is lovely. Ever since I was little, I always used to dream about sitting down with a bunch of mates talking about the complex dynamics between men and women.*

Ted Lasso has had an *interesting* night. He had a panic attack, he got divorced, and he had a one-night stand with a woman he just met (who happens to be Rebecca's best friend from her hometown). Now, he's sitting around with his friends talking it out.

Nathan sees the beauty in what they are doing, just being a group of friends. They care for one another and support each other. They are a group bonded together through love and friendship.

What is most surprising is that even though the group is comprised of people you wouldn't have expected, they each bring a unique voice and perspective to each issue they tackle. Those unique voices do not cancel one another out but lift up and support one another as they offer camaraderie and support to a friend in need.

Now, even though they are discussing Ted's (very recent) sex life, I imagine this group can and will get together to talk about all sorts of topics pertaining to life, love, and friendship.

- - - -

Whenever we talk about the disciples of Jesus, we often speak of them as simply *followers*. They follow the one they believe to be the Messiah. They abandon their previous lives and devote their new life to God. Their whole world centers around this man named Jesus.

However, the term we often neglect to bring up while talking about the disciples is that they are *friends*. They are a loving and close-knit group who cares about one another and supports each other. They each come from drastically different groups within their culture, but they see and cherish the value they have in one another.

Sure, there are still moments when they squabble, bicker, fight, and fail to see God at work among them, but that is typical of any group of friends. Despite those moments where they have differences, the majority of their time (that we know of) is spent in loving community with one another.

Everyone needs friends and people to share their life with. The life of faith that we live is not one of disparate lone rangers wandering the desert. The goal of our lives of faith is *not* to be the wise person sitting on the pinnacle of a mountain. Instead, our lives are intertwined and wrapped up in the people around us.

We are a gathered people – both as people of faith and as humanity as a whole. We seek counsel, fun, friendship, laughs, and more from others. Each person has a different level of comfort when it comes to group settings, but each of us still yearns to be a part of a group and a part of something whole.

It helps makes us complete. Yes, we still bicker and fight at times, but that exists in all group dynamics.

We live out this life of love and faith gathered with others. In this community of faith we are called into, we are invited to share with one another, support each other in truth and honesty, and celebrate and mourn together.

It *is* lovely to sit down with a bunch of mates and discuss the complexities of all that life has to offer.

The Gospel According to Ted Lasso

Jamie Starts to Get It

> **Jamie Tartt** – You also taught me to try to not get in me own way so much. So... thank you for that.
> **Keeley Jones** – You're welcome, Jamie.

Jamie Tartt is that character in any show that you love to hate. He gets on your nerves because he's so full of himself that he constantly thwarts his own progress. Whenever he begins to turn a corner in his own emotional and maturity development, he throws obstacles in his way so that he continues to stay in the same place. It's a place he is comfortable with, but a place that is so grating to everyone around him.

As the season of *Ted Lasso* has progressed, Jamie begins to see that there are indeed so many people around him that want the best for him. As he begins to see that letting others share in greatness isn't a *bad* thing, he understands that it helps him be a better person and a more complete footballer.

In his confession to Keeley, the cracks of his false bravado begin to show. He begins to finally be *real* and not just a caricature that he has created. He is thankful not only for what she has done, but he begins to see the good that others have tried to show him and guide him towards.

This new Jamie can potentially do even more amazing things.

- - - -

There is a man who comes to Jesus by night[32] because he's curious and wary of what Jesus has proclaimed. He is a part of the religious leadership within that time, entering that space with Jesus to figure him out and to try to find some common ground between what he's always known and what new things Jesus brings to the table.

We meet Nicodemus early in John's gospel, and he is only briefly

---
[32] John 3:1-21

mentioned two other times in that story. His story culminates at Jesus' trial and death. Nicodemus (along with Joseph of Arimathea) tends to Jesus' body. They help provide the means to give Jesus a proper and rightful burial.

Now, that doesn't mean that Nicodemus believed in *everything* that Jesus proclaimed. We don't hear from him again in scripture, but we have been witness to him periodically through John's gospel and can see how his opinion of the one who claims to be Messiah has shifted.

It has shifted enough that he's willing to risk what others think about him (and his own prominent place within his culture and society) in order to tend to this 'criminal' and seemingly failed prophet's body.

In each of our journeys in faith, we come to terms with all that we have been taught and what we have seen and experienced. As we encounter scripture and God active at work in the world, we cannot help but be changed. Sometimes that change helps us dive deeper into the faith we've always had; while there are other times where that encounter reshapes who we are and how we see the world.

Encountering Jesus does that to everyone, especially when the Jesus we are shown is the one who cares, loves, and sees worth in the people around him. How could we not change when encountered by that radical love?

STORIES

> **Ted Lasso** – You know, Rupert, guys have underestimated me my entire life. And for years, I never understood why. It used to really bother me. But then one day, I was driving my little boy to school and I saw this quote by Walt Whitman and it was painted on the wall there. It said, "Be curious, not judgmental."

This darts scene may be one of the most pivotal moments in the entire show of *Ted Lasso*. In this moment, Ted is 'standing up' for Rebecca against her ex-husband. It is a wonderful moment, not because of Ted's chivalrous actions, but because we get to learn a bit more of why Ted is the way he is, and he gets to 'stick it' to one of the main antagonists in this show.

He tells a story, a short story, about his life. And the crux of that story is that life is way more interesting when you're *curious* about people as opposed to judgmental or assuming towards them. Ted mentions that no one asks him questions, they just assume they are better than him.

Asking questions might've helped Rupert a bit in this dart game. Asking questions might have made him a little more cautious and less arrogant towards Ted. It wouldn't have guaranteed a win or a loss, but he would've learned more about the man he was competing against.

For Ted, learning about another person is the prize worth more than gold.

- - - -

Jesus liked to share stories. Many of the stories that Jesus shared were unconventional, but they helped show how Jesus viewed the world and how God was active and continues to be at work in the world.

Stories have a way of making something more real, more relevant, and more personable. In the stories that people tell, we become curious as to who this person is; we want to know more.

Jesus asked those questions as well. He wanted to know more and more about the people he interacted with. His stories ask questions of those listening, questioning the true intentions of others. Jesus' stories proclaimed God at work in the world, inviting others to be more curious about this message and love.

Whether he was sharing a story about a shepherd and his flock, having conversation at night with a skeptic, encountering a man possessed, or even asking for some water from a woman at a well, he was *curious* about the people he was with.

Jesus never shamed them into belief but offered questions and stories that helped them – and all of us – see ourselves in the midst of God's love. Living a life of curiosity isn't always easy because it is far less difficult to be judgmental. Remaining judgmental doesn't take any work; it doesn't require any change.

Living a life of curiosity helps us understand, learn from, and better live with those around us. Being curious and not judgmental requires work, patience, and grace. It isn't always easy, but a curious life is one filled with wonder and hope.

DISCUSSION QUESTIONS

- How do you define community?
    - Does that definition change if it is a community of faith?
- What are those moments in your life when you need to talk about it with your friends?
    - Are those moments mostly positive or negative? Why?
- When is a time that your view about something changed because of a conversation and/or relationship another person?
- How important are stories to convey truths in our lives?
    - Why or why not?
- How can you be 'curious, not judgmental' in your own life?

11
ALL APOLOGIES

FORGIVENESS

> **Rebecca Welton** – *Ted, I'm so sorry.*
> **Ted Lasso** – *Mm.*
> **Rebecca** – *If you want to quit or call the press, I'll completely understand.*
> **Ted** – *I forgive you.*

As Ted tells Rebecca, divorce is hard. When we are hurting, we tend to hurt others. It doesn't make it right, but it does give a reason as to *why* we sometimes hurt others in our lives. Hurting people, hurt people.

Rebecca is hurting. In her grief and anger about her marriage and divorce, she has hurt a lot of people. But, through it all she was only concerned about hurting one person – Rupert Mannion. She's hurt Ted, she's hurt Higgins, she's hurt Jamie, she's hurt Keeley, and she's hurt countless AFC Richmond fans.

Ted has the full right to hurt her back. No one would object to it. No one would fault him for it. Instead, he does the thing that might be the most difficult thing to do in the world. He forgives her. He understands the hurt she's dealing with – even if her coping mechanism was wildly wrong.

This episode doesn't just deal with Rebecca's apology and needed forgiveness, but involves Ted's too. Ted continues to fail to see how his insistence of always seeing the positive side of things might not be helpful or realistic. Losing 'doesn't' matter to him but losing is real.

Losing is real for this team and its fanbase. It's real for each of these players. Losing has consequences. Coach Beard helps Ted begin to see that.

Roy needs to apologize as well, needing to forgive himself. For almost his entire life, he has seen himself solely as a footballer. It is difficult for him to imagine that anyone could see him in any other way. Keeley helps him recognize that he is *more* than just a footballer, and he always has been. Her love and care for him (not to mention his niece's love of him) has nothing to do with how well he plays a game. Roy's forgiveness is him recognizing that he is more than just someone who can kick a ball really well.

- - - -

Forgiveness is hard. It's hard to give, and most of the time it's hard to receive.

Many of us don't ever feel worthy enough to receive forgiveness, and many of us don't think we are strong enough to give it to those who've hurt us. But, holding on to that grudge, that anger, those terrible emotions don't help us at all. They continue to hurt us and feed us with an energy that helps no one.

For me, forgiveness is as if you're holding on to a small cup of water. In the moment, that cup is rather light. We're okay holding on to that cup for a little bit. But imagine continuing to hold that cup, for minutes, hours, days, weeks, months, or years. The longer you grasp that cup the heavier it becomes. Your entire body becomes rigid and exhausted as it devotes energy to holding that cup. All your emotions and decisions are directly affected by that cup. The only way we can continue holding it is to be angrier and angrier at that cup, at our situation, at life because of that cup.

Forgiveness is taking that cup and letting go, setting it down. Forgiveness means that you're no longer going to let that action of another have power over you any longer. You're freeing yourself from that action.

Forgiveness *doesn't* mean that things have to or must go back to the way they were before. Forgiveness doesn't mean you go back to a hostile or abusive relationship. Forgiveness means that you *let go*.

Ted lets go of the anger that he could have towards Rebecca. Rebecca lets go of the anger she has towards Higgins. Ted and Roy are able to forgive themselves as they see one another grow into who they can be.

In scripture, we are reminded that God remembers our sin no more. It's gone. It doesn't play a role in how God sees you. Ever. You are forgiven. Always. Forever. Now.

Forgiveness is hard. However, anger can't be sustained forever; put that cup down and live.

Discussion Questions

- When was the last time you really forgave someone?
- When was the last time someone really forgave you?
- Why do you think it is difficult for us to forgive people?
- What does it mean for you to know that God really forgives you?
    - Are there moments where you truly believe that?
    - Are there moments when it is more difficult to believe in that type of forgiveness from God?

12
THE HOPE THAT KILLS YOU

HOPE

> **Ted Lasso** – *You're acting like we lost the game already, yeah? Why don't you have a little hope?*
> **Mae** – *Aw, Ted. Haven't you lived here long enough to realize? It's the hope that kills you.*

It has come to that pivotal match that will determine AFC Richmond's future. Will they stay in the Premier League, or will they be relegated to the Champion's League? Everyone is on pins and needles about what the future may hold, but most are feeling a sense of dejection. They believe that there is *no hope* for what is to come. The players and fans find it hard to believe that they have a chance.

In all likelihood, it appears they have no chance. Manchester City is faster, stronger, and more talented. There is no sense in believing in hope because that will only set you up for failure.

When things are going downhill, it is hard to hold on to hope.

And yet, Ted is trying to find anything, even if it is only a small straw to grasp which will encourage his team to play with hope. Ted wants his team to finally grasp what he has been trying to teach them all season; to believe.

As you look out into the world, there are moments, times, and events that don't seem very hopeful or hope-filled.

There is anger and division between people. There is the sense of doom regarding climate change. There continues to be a gulf between the haves and have nots that just seems to get wider and wider.

If you ask people what they hope in, you'll get a lot of answers. I fear that many of those answers would be sad, dejected, and more. Many people live without hope.

There are numerous moments within scripture where people lived without hope as well. Abraham and Sarah yearning for a child, Noah's family hoping the flood waters would recede, the Israelites held in slavery, and those who followed Jesus as they witnessed his death to name a few examples.

In each of those moments (and more) there appeared to be no hope. Yet, in spite of that absence of hope, there was still trust and belief that God would do *something*.

Those people didn't 'give up' and cease to live or function. They continued on, striving for that hope, working in that hope, looking towards that hope, trusting that God would provide – through and with their actions.

As people of faith, we cling to hope – however small it might seem at times. We hope that God is present in our lives. We hope that we are being led to a time where we can live into and be a part of the kingdom of heaven. We trust in God.

It isn't always easy. There are numerous obstacles thrown our way. But we trust. As Ted Lasso would say, we 'believe in believe.'

God is here. Christ is with us. The Spirit is guiding. Always.

Chaos Hammer

> **Ted Lasso** – All right, guys. Tell you right now, we're gonna go out there, and we're gonna learn a bunch of these plays, you hear? Come Sunday, we're gonna hit Man City with the Chaos Hammer!
> **Players** – Yeah!
> **Ted** – Let's go!

That shred of hope that Ted wants his team to cling to happens to be an unconventional one. He understands that Manchester City might be more talented in every tangible aspect of the game than his team, but that talent is only apparent when a traditional game of football is being played.

He hopes that causing confusion on the pitch will help even the playing field between these two teams. He asks his athlete's advice to give him all the trick plays that they have ever learned in their years of playing.

This moment is the pinnacle of Ted's coaching philosophy. Ted doesn't wish his team to play in such a way to cause confusion and frustration in the other side, but he expects his team to offer solutions and *be a part* of the process. By asking his players to offer up different trick plays, they are more invested than ever before.

Above all, whether they win or lose, they are going to play till the end and have *fun* doing it too.

- - - -

Jesus tells an odd parable in Luke's gospel where he praises a *dishonest* manager[33] for being shrewd. It is weird to hear Jesus tell a story where a person is somewhat 'lifted up' for fudging the numbers of the accounting book.

But, I don't think that is necessarily what Jesus is commending. What he is commending is that this man (selfishly or not) is *helping* others. He's

---
[33] Luke 16:1-13

cutting their debts so that when he does get let go (and for all intents and purposes he is) there will be more incentive for those to help him.

Playing a game of football full of trick plays will make any traditionalist rage. It isn't 'how the game is supposed to be played' they'll say, and for the most part, they are correct. When things are done outside the expected norm it is frustrating.

Yet, here we have Jesus lifting up an individual doing just that.

Sometimes you need to work in the ways of the world in order for God's light and grace to shine through ever more clearly. God directs us to work through the systems the world has put in place to offer hope, love, and care to those in need.

It might cause confusion for the powers that be in the world, but it brings life to those who need it most.

God is She

> ***Ted Lasso*** *– No, I hate ties, Nate. How many times I gotta tell you that? They ain't natural, all right? If God wanted games to end in a tie, she wouldn't have created numbers, all right?*

As the coaching and managerial staff is developing a sound gameplan for the match against Manchester City, we get to learn a little more about Ted. We, of course, know that he is not a sports fan who enjoys ties. For most sports in America, ties just don't exist. His reasoning for not being agreeable to ties is both fun and profound.

God invented numbers, so there shouldn't be ties.

What you might miss is that he identifies God as *she*. That's big. That's important.

It shows that Ted *does not* look at the world the way that many do. The way he interprets the world is *not wrong*, even if it is *different*.

- - - -

Listen. God is more than just one gender. God always has been. From the beginning of Genesis[34] humanity was created in the image of God – male and female. Within that part of scripture, God is most accurately referred to as *they*, *our*, and *them*.

As a person of faith who identifies as a Christian, our concept of the divine is in the Trinity. This Trinity is comprised of three sperate, but co-equal beings – God, Son, and Spirit.

Jesus at times refers to himself as a *mother hen* – one who gathers her chicks in love and protection.

---

[34] Genesis 1:26

Throughout scripture the Spirit or Wisdom of God is referred to as *she*.

God is not exclusively male or female. God is both and neither.

Opening ourselves to an interpretation of God that *isn't* male doesn't make us wrong or bad. But, it does help us see the intrinsic and deep value of *all genders*. For far too long we have seen being masculine as 'good and proper' when it comes to things of religion and faith and that feminine qualities are 'less than' in some way.

In this small, seemingly throwaway line, we continue to see Ted as one who sees the world as fuller and more open than others. That is a gift, not something to be dismissed or squashed. Perhaps, if we too were able to interpret life in that way, we would be surprised - in all the best ways – in how God shows up in places we wouldn't and didn't expect.

Not Alone

> ***Ted Lasso*** *– Look at everybody else here. And I want you to be grateful that you're going through this sad moment with all these other folks. Because I promise you, there is something worse out there than being sad, and that is being alone and being sad. Ain't nobody in this room alone.*

The show about a sports team has ended in a way that shows about sports teams don't typically end. AFC Richmond lost. They've been relegated. They won't be playing with the best teams in the United Kingdom in their next season.

Everyone is heartbroken. They came so close, and the old saying of that community came to pass – the hope has 'killed' them. They tied the game only to see that light of hope seemingly snuffed out in the last few seconds as Jamie Tartt made the extra pass to knock out his former team.

Now, after the game, Coach Lasso begins to do what he does best, *coach his team* through this moment. He recognizes their reality. He gives space for their mourning and grief. He asks them to look to the future; a future that is unwritten and unknown. He gives them space for a new future they can make the best of *as long as* they remember that though they are sad (and justifiably so) they are not *alone.*

This team, *his team*, is not alone. They have one another to share in their grief. They have one another to hold onto and lift one another up as they move forward with their goal; to make it back to the Premier League. Ted offers them the opportunity to become not just a better *team*, but a *community* of friends who love one another, support each other, and help make each person better for the good of the whole.

They are not, have not, and will not ever be alone. That realization of not being alone is the hope that will help them survive and thrive.

Whenever I have the honor of leading a funeral for my community, I like to tell those who are grieving that during that service we get to do three things.

First, we get to mourn. God has created us with emotion and all of those emotions come out as we grieve our loss. We are sad, sometimes angry, and many times we are confused. Yet, we are given space to live into and live out those emotions. We are given space to *mourn*. It is okay for us to do that. It is *good* for us to do that.

Second, we get to remember. We get to remember the life of the person we love. We get to share their stories, laugh, and celebrate the life we were able to share together. We get to listen to the stories and soak up all those ways that the one we mourn has connected a community together. It is okay for us to do that. It is *good* for us to do that.

Finally, we get to remember that this is *not* the end. For we have faith that we will see one another again. We get to remember that there is not one thing that can separate us from the love of God in Christ our Lord – not even death itself. We get to remember the promise and the gift of the resurrection. We get to remember that even in this moment the person we miss is not alone. We get to remember that in this grief and sadness *we are not* alone.

Throughout our scriptures, time and again, our God has reminded creation that we are not alone. We have been reminded that God is *with* us. We are remembered. Hope is still very much alive.

In the beginning of the Gospel of Matthew[35], Joseph is told in a dream that the child to be born to his fiancé would be called Emmanuel – God with us. This child is to be a reminder to all of creation that life is not lived alone. We are never alone, for God *is with* us. The ending of that Gospel[36] drives this point further home as just before Jesus ascends and departs

---

[35] Matthew 1:23
[36] Matthew 28:20b

from the disciples, he reminds them again of who he is. He is Emmanuel. He has been with them and he *will* be with them. Always.

We are not alone.

As Coach Lasso says, there is something worse than being sad – being sad and being alone. None of us are alone. Our God works through others, works through each of us, reminding all of creation that we are not alone.

We are surrounded by communities of all types, we are connected through the vastness and closeness of the internet, and we get to live life with others. God is with us. God hears our cries. God has come to live among us. God has been made known in creation so that we might all remember.

We are not alone. You are not alone. No one is alone.

Care for, lean into, and love on one another. Our God invites us into that holy work. Remember always, *Emmanuel*. God is with us.

DISCUSSION QUESTIONS

- What makes having hope difficult?
- What makes having hope easy?
- Where in the world now do you see God being shrewd to proclaim the Gospel?
  - Why?
- When someone has a different interpretation of faith than you do, is it easier or more difficult to be open to them? Why?
- How does it feel for you when you are alone?
- What are some ways that help you feel together and a part of something?
- What things have you done to show someone that they are not alone?
- How do you react when things don't go the way you wanted?

ABOUT THE AUTHOR

Rev. Matthew Titus is an ordained minister of Word and Sacrament in the Evangelical Lutheran Church in America. Currently he serves as the pastor of The Lutheran Church of The Redeemer in South Carolina. He lives with his wife and their two children.

Made in United States
Troutdale, OR
07/02/2023

10934731R00072